# THE MAKING

## OF A

# SOUTHERN INDUSTRIALIST

*Simpson Bobo Tanner*

# THE MAKING OF A SOUTHERN INDUSTRIALIST

*A Biographical Study of Simpson Bobo Tanner*

BY
GERALD W. JOHNSON

CHAPEL HILL  The University of North Carolina Press

Copyright 1952
BY THE UNIVERSITY OF NORTH CAROLINA PRESS

CMT

## ACKNOWLEDGMENT

Without the work of the late Maude Minish Sutton in assembling the biographical material this study would have been long delayed, if it had been possible at all. To her memory, therefore, and to the living, including members of the Tanner family, who have assisted the work, the writer acknowledges his debt.

GERALD W. JOHNSON

Baltimore
November, 1951

# Chronology

| | |
|---|---|
| 1853 | December 8, Simpson Bobo Tanner born near Clifton, South Carolina, to Andrew (1820-1898) and Ann Caroline Cannon Tanner (1835-1882) |
| 1870-73 | Clerked in McNally's store, Union, South Carolina |
| 1873-74 | Attended Bryant & Stratton Business College, Baltimore, Maryland |
| 1874 | On railway construction job |
| 1874-86 | With Elias & Cohen, jobbers |
| 1886 | Became associated with J. S. Spencer, banker |
| 1887 | Founded Henrietta Mills |
| 1888 | December 20, married to Lola, daughter of Jesse Smitherman Spencer and Henrietta McRae Spencer. Children: |
| | Kenneth Spencer, born May 30, 1890, married Sarah Huger Bacot |
| | Sara Henrietta, born April 30, 1893, married Dr. Robert Hope Crawford |
| | Simpson Bobo, junior, born February 5, 1895, died September 23, 1949, married Mildred Millicent Miller |
| | Jesse Spencer, born August 31, 1902, died November 4, 1923, unmarried |

| | |
|---|---|
| 1889 | Organized Florence Mill at Forest City, North Carolina |
| 1906 | Purchased control of Cleghorn Mill, Rutherfordton, North Carolina |
| 1907 | President, American Cotton Manufacturers' Association |
| 1907 | Organized Green River Mill, at Tuxedo, North Carolina |
| 1917 | Sold interest in Henrietta Mills |
| 1920 | February 22, Lola Spencer Tanner died |
| 1921 | Sold Florence Mills |
| 1923 | November 4, Jesse Spencer Tanner died |
| 1924 | July 3, Simpson Bobo Tanner died. Buried in Elmwood Cemetery, Charlotte, North Carolina, beside his wife and youngest son |

# THE MAKING

## OF A

## SOUTHERN INDUSTRIALIST

# *Simpson Bobo Tanner*

SIMPSON BOBO TANNER DID NONE OF the things that schoolboys think are necessary to make a man a historical figure. But he made history. He held no high political office, he commanded no armies, he explored no jungles, he produced no famous books, plays, pictures, or operas. He was merely a business man. Yet if the schoolboy happens to live in North Carolina, or anywhere in the South, his life is different from what it would have been without the Tanners of the period right after the Civil War; and whoever changes things for many people makes history.

We all admit that such men as Jefferson Davis and Robert E. Lee have had a profound effect upon succeeding generations; but we seldom stop to realize that we understand their effectiveness because what they did was dramatic. Law-making and war-making are important, but they are also spectacular; they not only change our lives, but they do it suddenly and sometimes violently, so it is impossible for us to overlook the changes or ignore the men who brought them about. It isn't the extent of the change that impresses us, it is the way in which it was done. Many men have altered the face of the world to a greater extent than any soldier or statesman, yet succeeding generations give them less attention than they give to such a soldier as Horatio Gates or such a President as Millard Fillmore, not to mention the really great rulers and warriors.

The result is that our knowledge of how we came to be what we are is frequently wrong and nearly always inadequate, because the history we study accounts for only part of the forces that moulded us.

To be specific, the development of North Carolina since the year 1865 covers changes so radical that they comprise a social, political, and economic revolution. The political phase of it has been dinned into our ears by campaign orators and partisan newspapers from our youth up; but only recently have we paid much attention to the social and economic phases, although they are at least twice as important as politics, if one's aim is to understand why things are as we find them today.

When S. B. Tanner was born, Rutherford County was a strictly agricultural region in a country that was rapidly being industrialized, which is to say, its economy was badly adjusted to the times. When he died the county was well to the front in industrialization, and its economic status, already good, was steadily improving. This was his work to so large an extent that it would be no great distortion of the truth to carve, almost anywhere in the county, the inscription they carved in memory of Sir Christopher Wren in St. Paul's cathedral: *Si monumentum requiris circumspice*, "If you seek his monument, look around you."

The man should be understood by the modern generation. Note well that the word is "understood," not worshipped. Ancestor-worship has been one of the conspicuous failings of the South, accountable for a great many of its malaises, and while North Carolinians congratulate themselves that the affliction has been milder in their state than in some others, it has been quite prevalent enough between Murphy and Manteo to handicap the cultural development of the commonwealth. All too often our idea of paying adequate tribute to a successful man, particularly one whose success has brought him wealth, is to smear him with literary goosegrease—to ignore, even to deny, his human failings and to describe him as a perfect compound of nobility, sanctity, and wisdom.

Naturally, it is a disservice. Intelligent men take one look at the mess and dismiss the subject as unworthy of consideration. They know that no man was ever that good; so if the so-called tribute is obviously false in one respect, why should it be believed in anything? Thus in the end the man's real virtues, far from being celebrated, are more deeply obscured than ever.

Let this consideration of one of North Carolina's pioneer industrialists begin, then, with an emphatic repudiation of any purpose to list the man among the saints and sages. He was a decent citizen and he was intelligent; but this, which can be proved abundantly, is the limit of the claims that will be advanced here touching his moral and intellectual qualities. Nor did he create the North Carolina textile industry single-handed. He was not "the" industrialist, he was "an" industrialist of his period; but this does not diminish, it increases his significance, for by understanding Tanner a modern North Carolinian may make an approach to understanding a whole class of men and a whole economic revolution.

It would be difficult to demonstrate conclusively that he was the outstanding example even of his own group. He made a fortune in the cotton mill business, but other men have made greater ones. He introduced improvements in methods and machinery, but other men have made as many, or more. He developed economic, sociological, and political ideas that were striking and successful in his time, but that have long since been outmoded. In none of these respects is his career more deserving of the attention of this generation than the careers of half a dozen of his contemporaries.

But in one particular he is nearly, if not quite, unique; and it is a particular of exceptional value to anyone who wishes really to know North Carolina. He was integrated with the state to an extraordinary degree. By the accident of birth he was of South Carolina, but by ancestry and early training he was profoundly North Carolinian. His acquaintance with the state began literally with the soil, for he sprang from a race of tillers of the soil, and its mud and dust plastered him as a young traveling salesman. It is doubtful that he ever looked into the books of John Stuart Mill and Adam Smith, but he learned economics from droughts and floods, hailstorms, and insect pests in the Carolina Piedmont. The principles of credit he learned by trusting the wrong people (but not many). The perils of over-extension he learned by losing money. The theory of surplus value may never have crossed his mind, but the practice of surplus value was familiar to him before he was old enough to vote. All of it sprang from the red hills among which he was raised and by close and observant association with the people who laboriously scratched a living from those hills.

At the half-way point of the twentieth century this should be thoroughly understood by every North Carolinian, above all by young people, for the reason that it is being boldly denied. There is a superstition abroad, sedulously cultivated by critics of the South, that such people as Tanner never lived. The industrialization of the South—so runs the current mythology—was effected entirely by outsiders, mostly from New England, who moved in to batten on what was, in effect, peon labor. Some New Englanders have moved in, impressive numbers within the past twenty years; but the truth is that they had to move because they were driven from their original stronghold by the fierce, aggressive competition of Southern-born, Southern-bred industrialists heading a labor force that may have been in peonage but didn't know it and therefore was rapidly increasing in energy and efficiency.

Simpson Bobo Tanner is especially worthy of study because he was an almost perfect example of this type. Comprehend what he did, and you will know, not only how North Carolina was industrialized, but also to what an astonishing extent it raised itself by its own bootstraps, having already emerged from economic stagnation before New England discovered its existence.

This knowledge is highly valuable at a time when half the world seems to have adopted the attitude of Gloomy Gus, who is certain that all is lost, and that there is no power and no virtue left in us as a people. S. B. Tanner faced a far worse situation than ours, but he pulled out of it; if we can't do as much, under easier conditions, we shall fail not because the Russians are very terrible (or the labor unions, or the New Dealers, or the atheists, or what not—write your own ticket) but because we don't raise any more S. B. Tanners.

# 1

SIMPSON BOBO TANNER WAS BORN ON December 8, 1853,* just early enough to remember the beginning of the South's Time of Troubles, and to remember also the end of one of the early efforts at industrialism in the South.

This was the development of the Iron District, an area bounded roughly by a triangle drawn from High Shoals, in North Carolina, to Cherokee Falls, South Carolina, to Spartanburg, and back through Cowpens to High Shoals. It contained considerable deposits of low-grade ore which could then be worked at a profit, since the extremely high-grade ores of the Great Lakes district had not yet been brought into competition. In the Iron District

---
*Some of the records seem to make it 1852, but careful investigation by the family after his death fairly established 1853 as the correct date and it so appears on his grave marker.

prior to 1870 a number of furnaces had been established producing pig-iron by smelting with charcoal and, where water power was available, forging the metal into various commercial shapes.

Into this region, about 1841, went young Andrew Tanner, born in Rutherford County, North Carolina, of a family that had settled there in the latter part of the eighteenth century. Andrew, attaining the age of twenty-one, had been given a horse, a suit of clothes, five dollars, and his "freedom," according to the custom of the time—that is to say, his father relinquished any further claim to his services—and thus equipped, set out to make his fortune. At first, perhaps, he farmed a little, but it was not long until he found employment at one of the more important furnaces, that at Hurricane Shoals, where iron was wrought as well as smelted.

The proprietor of the Hurricane Shoals Iron Works was one Simpson Bobo, who was not merely an ironmaster, but a man of some consideration in public affairs. He was one of the signers of the Ordinance of Secession in 1860, and his descendants have played prominent roles in the region ever since. That he was an excellent employer is attested by the fact that Andrew Tanner stayed with him for close to thirty years; and that he was an amiable gentleman is certainly indicated by the fact that after eleven years' association—long enough to know the man thoroughly—Tanner named a son for him.

Andrew himself was far from a commonplace character. By the time war broke out in 1861 he had worked up to a position that was considered indispensable by the Confederate military authorities. As soon as war began, production of iron became a matter of vital importance, and to put an ironmaster in the army would have been the wildest kind of folly. Yet in order to be effective even behind the lines a man must have authority; so although they kept Tanner on the job they gave him a military title, and he was known as "Colonel" for the rest of his days.

Hurricane Shoals (now Clifton, South Carolina) boomed during the war, but soon after 1865 the whole Iron District fell upon evil days. Ores with a much higher content of iron were becoming available and the higher the content of iron the easier and cheaper it is to smelt. By 1870 the Carolina field could no longer compete and about that time the last of the workings was abandoned.

It was, however, no unique disaster. In one way or another, for one reason or another, the whole South was prostrate, and a fierce, relentless sifting of its human material took place. If a man's makeup included any serious element of weakness, physical or moral, he broke under the strain of that savage crisis and either died or drifted down into the ranks of the human derelicts. For decades the South was filled with these relics of former greatness whose mere existence cast a shadow of tragedy upon the land. William Faulkner has found them in the second and third generation even in the twentieth century.

But Andrew Tanner survived. When the industry in which he had spent most of his active life collapsed under him, although he was in his forties he bobbed up again. Immediately after the iron works folded it seems likely that the Colonel had a very hard time. There are no records to show exactly how he lived, but he did live; and presently the records show him again, no longer as an ironmaster, but as a railroad contractor. He built part of the old Carolina Central, between Charlotte and Wadesboro; apparently he built part of one line from Charlotte south, and he was one of the men responsible for the brilliant engineering feat of carrying the railroad line up Saluda Mountain.

It is in no way surprising to find in the son of such a man courage, energy, and resolution, for the father had these qualities to a marked degree. He in turn had inherited them, for his grandfather, S. B. Tanner's great-grandfather, had made the long trek down from Pennsylvania toward the end of the eighteenth century, first into Virginia and then into what was almost unbroken wilderness, now Rutherford County. There, the family had hewed out a homestead that pushed civilization a little farther west. The Tanners were of German stock—the name seems to have been Donner originally—but English and Scotch-Irish strains had been mingled with the German after a few generations in America. However, it was all pioneer blood, which shows at its best when the going gets tough.

It was excessively tough when Simpson Bobo Tanner was a boy—how tough the modern generation can imagine only with difficulty, if at all. It was not merely that after 1865 everybody in North Carolina was poor. The money loss was only a part, and a relatively unimportant part of it. Civilization had crashed. When the boy reached the age of puberty North Carolina was not even a state, but merely part of a military district, and he had reached the age of adolescence before it regained its place in the Union. He was well beyond his legal majority before the whole South was clear of the Army of Occupation.

The past was gone forever—economically, politically, culturally. Slaves were lost, money was lost, property, except land, was almost totally lost. But more than that, and worse than that, all the social and political ideas and traditions that had been instilled into the Southern people from their youth up were no longer valid in the new situation. And the educational system was prostrate, so that the means of fitting themselves out with a new set of ideas did not exist. This meant that to all human appearances the future was lost, too.

Half a century later, after the war of 1917-19, there was much talk in this country of the "lost generation" of young men who had fought in that war and emerged without faith, hope, or charity. But it was all vapid nonsense by comparison with the situation that faced Tanner and his contemporaries in the years immediately after 1865. There was a generation that really was lost, past, present, and future; and the fact that they found themselves and the way that they found themselves compose a story the South has largely ignored, but that is in reality as fine a part of its record as the Shenandoah Valley campaign or the splendor of the character of Lee.

The boy who is the subject of this sketch, for instance, faced the world, the highly competitive modern world, equipped with a total of three months' formal schooling. There were a few other scraps and fragments of class-room training; for instance, he spent two weeks in a kind of institution that has passed out of existence but that was familiar all over the country a century ago, a writing school.

It has passed out because we don't need it. Mark that fact, for the disappearance of many things that are no longer needed must be taken into account if one is really to understand the careers of such men as Tanner. Nowadays a steady wrist and well-controlled fingers are not especially valuable business assets because anyone not downright paralytic can write legibly on a typewriter. But in 1865 the ingenious Mr. Sholes was still monkeying with his invention, which he would not patent for three years, and a clerk who could not turn out readable script was of little use in a business office.

In two weeks Tanner learned, and he never forgot. Later, when he was a young man, he spent three months in a business college—Bryant and Stratton's, still in existence in Baltimore—where he picked up the elements of bookkeeping and general business practice. But counting in everything, it is doubtful that he spent the equivalent of a calendar year in school. In short, he started life without education in the sense of formal schooling.

Furthermore, he started at a moment when early, exact, and accurate information was becoming not merely desirable but essential to any business man who undertook to do more than a picayune local business. The years from the end of the Civil War to 1900 were years when the extension of American business interests was less like an expansion than an explosion. Industry was rushing headlong into new fields, and when anyone—an industrialist, an army commander, a scientist, or a philosopher—intrudes into a new field, the most valuable asset he can have is a large store of reliable information, precisely what this man lacked.

In sum, he began life with everything against him, every imaginable thing. He had no capital and small hope of getting any, for the country around him was denuded of capital. He had no experience, he had no education, he had small hope of outside assistance, for he was one of the official outcasts. He belonged to a defeated nation that was suffering the rigors of a vengeful administration that had repudiated the rational statecraft of Lincoln, insistent on bandaging and salvaging the wounds of the nation, and had adopted instead the venomous politics of Thad Stevens, perfectly willing to sacrifice a third of the country in order to win an election.

The way in which he pulled through in spite of his handicaps is the one part of Tanner's story that is strictly individual. Other men at the same time and in similar circumstances adopted other methods, each guided by his particular experience;

but even this highly personal phase of his story contains, if not a guide for the modern generation, at least a number of highly suggestive hints, not in the specific things that he did, but in the attitudes he developed toward problems and people. The things that he did are, in many cases, impossible to repeat because conditions have changed; but the spirit in which he went about making a career was not dependent upon time and circumstance, but developed from the man's own character and intelligence and therefore may be copied by any other man who is endowed with the same degree of integrity and acumen.

# 2

THE FIRST BREAK CAME WHEN ONE McNally, a merchant in Union, South Carolina, offered the eighteen-year-old boy a job clerking in his store. It was not much of a break, even for those times, and to a modern youth it might seem less like a break than like a sentence to penal servitude. The hours were from sunrise to two hours after dark—pretty close to a hundred-hour week —and the compensation consisted of a bed in the store, meals with the storekeeper's family, and $100 a year, payable on New Year's Day.

But to young Tanner in 1870 it seemed to be a golden opportunity. It is probable that most boys of his age in his neighborhood would have felt the same way, which is eloquent of conditions on

Southern farms five years after the end of the Civil War.

Recently it has become fashionable to lament the industrialization of the South as having destroyed the sturdy yeomanry that drew virtue and strength from contact with the soil; but the lamenting is usually done by townsmen whose contact with the soil is limited to golf courses and small flower-gardens. When a farm boy of eighteen would jump at a chance to work fourteen hours a day for $100 a year rather than continue on the farm, it is evident that farm life must have been pretty grim. Even if the arrangement provided, as there is some reason to believe, for an increase of $100 for each consecutive year that the boy stayed with McNally, still the job was no sinecure. Rural life in North Carolina is far better today; but it is futile to try to understand a man like Tanner by assuming that what he did in 1870 was done under the conditions existing in 1950.

The fact is that he enjoyed working for McNally. "We had a lot of fun," said his friend, James McLaughlin, who got him the job and who was his fellow-clerk. It was probably more fun than Tanner had ever had before; and if that was the case, it is easy to see why he stuck to it for three years. In any event, although a man's condition may be very low indeed, if he is quite sure that he is on the rise, he is usually a reasonably happy man. The moment he got into McNally's store young Tanner—"Simps" to his associates—felt that he had taken the first step toward the improvement of his lot, and how far he had come was not nearly as important as the fact that he was on his way.

However, this very first step demonstrated two of the qualities that accounted for his success—foresight and resolution. Foresight assured him that he could not go very far with the intellectual equipment then in his possession; resolution enabled him to resist the temptation to spend every cent of his $100 a year—or his later $200, and finally $300—and to hold the greater part of it for the purpose of paying for better training.

But while looking forward to formal training by professionals he did not neglect the informal training that was to be had right there in the store. He became not merely a good clerk, but a very good one, so good that his ability was remembered long years after he had gone on to bigger jobs. McNally's clientele was pretty much that of country merchants all over the South. Most of them came from homes not unlike Tanner's own except that the majority of them were, if anything, poorer. McNally's clerk started with a pretty fair understanding of their needs, and he improved that understanding every day for three years. He ended knowing what such people wanted far better than most of them knew themselves. He knew the designs they liked, he knew the quality of goods they needed, and he knew the price they could pay.

So stated, this may look absurdly simple, but it is in fact the basic equipment of a great merchant. A customer is a customer and a salesman who can learn the needs of one can learn those of another, however different. Because S. B. Tanner was the kind of man who could, and did, learn thoroughly the needs of Piedmont Carolina farmers, he was capable of learning the needs of peasants in Manchuria, of herdsmen in the Pamirs, and of laborers in the sun-scorched fields east of Bombay. Some decades later Lancashire textile men were aghast to find S. B. Tanner outselling them in remote stretches of China and Tibet. They knew he had never set foot in Asia, and they were mystified, because it occurred to few if any of them that he had learned about poor yellow men by studying poor white men around his home. In the end, they did him the compliment of imitating his methods, especially of packing and shipping. It was one of the great satisfactions of his life to see the British following his lead.

All this, however, was a long time ahead of the young man who at twenty-one threw up a job at which he had been doing well in order to go back to school. But Tanner was resolute. He had gone to work for McNally for one purpose, namely, to collect a stake. Now he had it, thanks in part to a loan from his friend McLaughlin which, added to his savings, gave him money enough for a term in business school; so without a moment's hesitation he broke his connection at Union and late in 1873 left for Baltimore.

Some of the people around said he was crazy. Here was a young man with a good job who had proved himself one of the best clerks in the region and who had accumulated perhaps as much as $600. If he didn't want to work for McNally any longer, why not start in some kind of business for himself? Why spend every cent of that hard-earned money acquiring more book-learning which he might, or might not have a chance to use? Men who regarded themselves as hard-headed, practical fellows were inclined to shake their heads over the case of Simps Tanner.

But they lacked his foresight which, considering all the circumstances, was nothing to cause wonder, for his foresight was remarkable. At this time he had no idea what was to be his life's work. He knew that he was destined for a business career, but what kind he had not yet discovered. Yet he saw clearly that no business on a big scale could be operated by a man who knew nothing more than McNally's primitive methods. He was perfectly sure that he had a good mind, and he was shrewd enough to see that a good mind adequately trained would be worth a great deal more than the few hundred dollars that he and McLaughlin had scraped together. So he gambled everything he had on the theory that his brain was superior to his brawn. It was not for the last time, and bets of that kind he invariably won; but it is rather astonishing that a man so young with prospect so vague should be so confident. That, though, is undoubtedly one of the things that made him end as a business tycoon instead of a moderately successful small-town merchant.

In any event, he spent an extremely fruitful winter at Bryant and Stratton's. It goes without saying that a man who went to school with the sort of cool desperation that Tanner exhibited did not waste his time after he arrived. It is clear that he soaked up information like a sponge. Double-entry bookkeeping was his main acquisition, as far as the school catalogue was concerned, but this pupil got more than that. His subsequent career shows that he came back from Baltimore with a pretty clear understanding of the elements of accounting, a better than clear understanding of current business practice especially as regards office management, and a really remarkable grasp of the credit system especially in such details as commissions, discounts, and the management of commercial paper.

It is unnecessary to believe that he picked up all this between the late fall of 1873, when he went to Baltimore, and the early spring of 1874, when he returned to North Carolina. He did not. He merely started his commercial education in Baltimore and kept on learning for many years, indeed, one may say practically to the end of his life; for he never got too old to accept a new item of information with interest and to fit it into what he had known before. But in this winter he did learn the basic principles of the economic system, and thereafter it was merely a matter of building on that base with the aid of observation and intelligence.

On his return he found his father involved in the railroad-building enterprise between Charlotte and Wadesboro. Andrew Tanner needed a good office man, so Simps stepped into a ready-made job in which he could make excellent use of all his newly-acquired knowledge. But it was a temporary job. He knew that when the construction work was finished he would have to look around for something else; so he began looking at once.

The opportunity was not long in coming. Before the year 1874 was out Elias and Cohen, a jobbing concern, needed a man for their Charlotte house. Someone told them that Colonel Andrew Tanner had a son who was looking for a business opportunity and they promptly made him an offer at $30 a month. As a matter of human interest it should be recorded that Elias and Cohen had never heard of Simps Tanner, and they were not at all impressed by the fact that he had been to a business college. They hired him because they knew Andrew Tanner, and they figured that any son of his was bound to have good stuff in him. How right they were was shown promptly. Tanner never drew $30 a month. At the end of his second month the firm raised him to $50 and made it retroactive; so, although he did not know it at the time, from the very beginning he worked at the higher rate.

The next twelve years were very important, perhaps supremely important, in the life of Simpson Bobo Tanner, and yet there is less to record concerning them than is to be found about almost any other period. It is clear that during this period the man made some money—ten thousand dollars or so—but that is nearly all that can be stated definitely. Yet the most superficial examination of the record leads to the inference that the money he saved was the least of his acquisitions while he worked for Elias and Cohen; for he entered their service a young countryman, smart without doubt, but, as regards the ways of the world, pretty much uncurried and uncombed; and he emerged from their service with every one of the qualities that made him a great business man already developed. All that he still lacked was capital, which is not a quality but an instrumentality.

This is the sort of thing that drives biographers to drink, but it happens with reference to practically every man of eminence whose life is subjected to study. Frequently it is a matter of relative ease to trace all the side issues, all the subsidiary forces that contributed to his making—ancestry, education, social environment, economic status—which are, or may be, written down in public and private records, or at least stored in the memories of contemporaries. But there will always be found at least a dozen other boys with the same ancestry, education, environment and the rest, who never did anything remarkable; therefore it is evident that in the eminent man there is some additional factor, not recorded in family Bibles, school records, business ledgers, or the archives at the county courthouse, and, as a rule, never perceived by his contemporaries.

Yet this is precisely the thing that made him what he was, that differentiated him from the rest, that explains why he, and not the others, made a mark in the world that leads us to believe that it is necessary to understand him. This factor is the development of his powers, which the biographer has to explain largely by inference and hypothesis, or to put it bluntly, by guess-work; and this is one reason why there is so much bad biography in the world.

Tanner's case is perhaps less baffling than most, for at least we know the period during which he attained mastery, and we know how his outward life was conducted at that time; thus we have some foundation of solid fact on which to erect an inferential account of his inner life.

The first of these facts is that he is known to have been a thumping success as a salesman with Elias and Cohen. The way they raised his salary is proof enough; but, in addition to that, people could remember a generation later the amazing way in which Simps Tanner handled the wagon trade, that is, country merchants who, at intervals usually dictated by the seasons, drove big covered wagons to the market town to renew their stocks. Railroad transportation was still embryonic; so these men hauled the stuff themselves from the nearest trading center, which was Charlotte.

Most of them were pretty much like McNally, and Tanner had not worked for McNally for three years without learning both the man and the store.

He knew the merchants. He knew the merchants' customers back in the country. He knew Elias and Cohen's stock. Therefore he knew how to sell the merchant the kind of stock that would satisfy his trade. More than that—and here, no doubt, we touch one of the man's really essential qualities—he was never blinded by greed; he would not, in order to better his own sales record, "oversell," that is, persuade a merchant to buy more goods than he could reasonably hope to dispose of readily. In a short time the country merchants found that what they bought from Tanner moved smoothly; so they sought him out whenever they came to town.

More than that, they liked him personally. Tall, ruddy, although his hair and mustache were dark rather than blond, and affable, he was a fine figure of a man. And he talked their language. There was nothing in the life of the farms and villages of the Piedmont that he didn't know all about. Curiously, he lacked one great asset of most successful salesmen and politicians—he was not good at remembering names. But he was a famous story-teller and his interest in the problems of the merchants and their people was unfeigned. They were his people, and they knew that he was one of them.

Such a man could not long be confined to the display rooms and warehouses in Charlotte. He was too valuable as a contact-maker; so within a relatively short time he was put on the road as traveling representative of the company, a "drummer" in the parlance of the day.

Here again it is necessary to make a conscious effort to penetrate the barrier that time and change have dropped between us and the world of 1880. Even today "the road" is not a bed of ease, yet a man can endure it without having the physical stamina of a first-rate athlete. But when Tanner started out, his six-foot frame and the iron-hard muscles that his boyhood labor in the fields had developed were important parts of his equipment for the job. His territory included Rutherford, Polk, and Henderson counties, as well as some less formidable areas in both Carolinas. Rutherford, Polk, and Henderson are rugged country today, but luxuriously easy by comparison with what they were eighty years ago. Rail transportation was out, except for a few stretches so short that they hardly counted. Nine-tenths of the salesman's travel was behind horses, usually in a top-buggy exactly like those in which the parson and the doctor rode except that the salesman's had a longer box to accommodate his sample cases behind the seat.

The rider in a modern automobile has little conception of the strain to which the human frame was subjected by riding all day in such a vehicle, even on smooth roads; and the roads that Salesman Tanner traversed were beyond description. Inches deep in powdery dust in summer, hub-deep in red mud in winter, seldom cleared of rocks and roots capable of producing jolts that would smash felloes and spokes and bend axletrees, to say nothing of precipitating an unwary driver to the ground, they were a test of strength, endurance, and driving skill such as the average motorist has never imagined, much less experienced.

It took a strong man, a well-nigh indestructible man, to survive that kind of travel day after day, year after year, and to arrive at his destination jolly, good-humored, full of gay and amusing stories, and capable of making a vigorous and effective sales talk. But one who did survive, and who was capable of reflection, learned much. Tanner survived and learned. Among other things he learned very early to avoid the most dangerous trap that lies in the way of men who follow a nerve-racking and bone-racking way of life, the excessive use of alcohol. Few men really felt the need of a drink more than did the traveling salesman of 1880 at the end of his day's journey, and it was fatally easy for the drink to double and triple and quadruple itself until presently the man became a sot. This tendency Tanner resisted with a vigor that made him, if never quite a fanatic, yet decidedly rigid on the subject when he became an employer of large numbers of workmen.

Here, too, he must have acquired an abiding respect for the difficulties of transportation in a region with few, if any, well-built roads. Years later, when he was fighting for foreign markets, and men explained to him about camel trains across the Gobi, or the use of llamas in Peru, or yaks in Tibet, he could understand because he had seen pack animals often enough in the mountains of North Carolina. Therefore if a customer desired goods made up in packages small enough for a llama to carry, he could comprehend the reasonableness of the request, which some American manufacturers were never able to do.

There is one other well-attested fact that is significant of Tanner's development in this period. It is the deal by which he began to make really important money; yet its real significance is not the money it made then, but the attitude it revealed. The deal lasted for a few years only, but the attitude remained and accounts for vastly larger successes later.

Elias and Cohen were carrying a line of coarse domestic sheeting and some plaid shirtings on which the profit margin was very thin, so thin that the firm decided to drop both as not worth the trouble of handling. But both were desired in

Tanner's territory. Both were useful to the people of the hill country. Both were right in quality and in price. Therefore to supply them was a service of value to those people.

Accordingly, Tanner and one other salesman asked Elias and Cohen for permission to carry these lines on the side, as personal ventures. The firm had no objection and even permitted the salesmen to invoice the stuff through their office, provided they would compensate the bookkeeper for his extra trouble. But Cohen, the partner in charge of the Charlotte house, thought it only fair to warn the young men that they were taking a considerable risk. The profit on that sheeting, for example, hardly ran to a dollar on a thousand yards and one bad credit risk might easily put a whole season's business in the red.

Tanner, however, felt that if his customers wanted goods of a certain kind, it was his business as a salesman to find those goods at a price they could pay. The profit margin was less important than the service, because the service would establish good-will. Then and there the man ceased to be a salesman and became a merchant, not because he was buying and selling on his own account, but because he was purveying service as well as merchandise.

Thirty years later Edward A. Filene, the great

Boston merchant, built a whole philosophy of retail trade—and, incidentally, a famous store—on this very idea. Doubtless there is some profit in the mark-up, said Filene, but the largest attainable profit is not in the mark-up at all, it is in the business policy of giving the customer the goods that he needs at a price that he can pay; and the genius of the merchant is not in persuading the customer to buy, but in finding goods of the right quality at the right price.

Tanner never thought this all out and put it in a book as Filene did, but he was practicing it when Filene was still an adolescent in his father's small specialty shop. Since Elias and Cohen would not handle the stuff, he went out looking for it and found it in the product of a local concern, the Montgomery Mills. Incidentally, he found a mentor in Captain John H. Montgomery, a former merchant who had gone into manufacturing, but who retained a vivid interest in markets. This Tanner, himself engaged in merchandising, could understand; and it is easy to believe that Montgomery had something, perhaps much, to do with the bent of his mind in later years.

The sheeting-and-shirting deal turned out much more handsomely than anyone had expected. What Cohen failed to allow for was Tanner's amazingly thorough knowledge of his territory. He just didn't take bad credit risks. He knew to a dollar how much could be sold by the smallest country store in the remotest cove in the hills, and he allowed the proprietor his quota and no more. Yet he did it so good-humoredly, so reasonably, that he offended nobody and many of the merchants came to the point at which they would say, when he walked in, "Take a look at the shelves and sell me what I need." So, even at a profit margin of only a dollar a thousand yards, he cleaned up. Presently both he and the bookkeeper were drawing as much from the side line as they were paid by Elias and Cohen.

Incidentally, in covering the whole region he became intimately acquainted with everything that was going on. He saw villages that were picking up and growing into towns. He knew where the really good farm land lay and when a desirable property came on the market; and he was, of course, a specialist on the credit rating of everybody in a hundred communities. So he was able now and then to turn a neat profit in real estate and to pick up something by discounting notes.

Still, he was not satisfied. He was prosperous, he was popular, and he was becoming a man of substance; but he felt that he was somehow in a backwater, not in the main current of events. The mainstay of Southern economy was cotton, and he who was not involved with cotton, in one way or another, was running a side-show. It might be profitable and it might be pleasant, but it was nevertheless a side-show, and Tanner wanted to be in the main tent.

His own explanation of his discontent was that he wanted more money, and that he wanted money was certainly true. But he was making money where he was, and he had every reason to suppose that by continuing he would make it faster and faster with less and less risk and exertion. The fact is that he wanted more than money. He wanted to play in the big league. He wanted to be where memorable things were being done. He wanted to be an important man, as well as a rich man. But this is not the spirit of a mere money-grubber. Acquisitive Tanner most certainly was, but to dismiss him as merely acquisitive is to forfeit all chance of really understanding him or what he did.

His whole generation has suffered by the failure of later writers to get below the superficial aspect of their careers. For the most part, they were inarticulate. They could explain that they desired a profit, but they could not explain what they desired over and above a profit—the indefinable satisfaction of building, of creating, of erecting a great structure where nothing was before. They made glaring mistakes and commentators too often have been content to attribute the mistakes entirely to the blindness of greed, whereas many of them really were due to an effort to attain a grandeur that was unattainable. Frequently they grew arrogant as age crept upon them, sometimes they became fanatical, but very few—one dare say none of the really big ones—developed into an Ebenezer Scrooge, miserly and miserable.

Transition to the cotton business was not difficult for any man engaged in merchandising, for every retail merchant in the country was more or less involved in it. Cotton was, in effect, the currency of the region, not quite to the extent that tobacco was in colonial Virginia, but very nearly. On the size and condition of his cotton crop depended a farmer's credit at the store. He lived on credit through winter, spring, and summer, and in the autumn settled his account, not with money, but with cotton. A merchant, therefore, did not last long unless he were a reasonably good judge of cotton, both as a crop in the field and as staple in the bale; and a traveling salesman, dealing with merchants, had to be as good a judge, or better. Long before he quit Elias and Cohen, Tanner, like every other first-rate salesman, was a first-rate judge of cotton.

The question was one of business connections.

Tanner was well-known and popular in Charlotte and at least half a dozen possibilities were open to him; but the one he chose was without doubt the best, from his point of view. The man with whom he became allied was J. S. Spencer. Perhaps the truth is that Spencer chose him, for at the time this former Confederate soldier, become by degrees merchant, manufacturer, and banker, was a power in the business world of Charlotte. To be invited to join forces with Spencer was, in the small business of a small town, almost what it was for a young business man in New York to be invited to become a partner in the house of Morgan. Spencer's success was, in fact, due very much to the quality that made the elder Morgan a colossus—ability to pick able young assistants.

In this case he picked, perhaps, more than he bargained for. He acquired, not merely a business associate, but a son-in-law. In any event, Tanner pleased the older man so much that the business connection soon became also a social one; Tanner was invited into the Spencer home repeatedly and very promptly fell victim to the charms of the third daughter of the house, Lola. Tradition has it that this was one of his toughest campaigns, for at first Lola was not much impressed. For one thing, Tanner was fourteen years her senior and his busy, hard-driving life had left him little time to cultivate the social graces. A young woman of great personal charm and a daughter of the town's leading citizen certainly had no lack of admirers, and it says much for Tanner's audacity that he raised his eyes to her. But he did, and it is evident that he went into this project with characteristic energy and determination. Even so, it took him two years to bring the lady to his way of thinking, and not until 1886 was their engagement announced.

Marriage in those days was no half-hearted affair. It was definite, permanent, and private. Not only was it expected to last, but it wasn't discussed. A man who said anything, good or bad, about his relations with his wife was assumed to be drunk, or losing his mind. So there is not much in the record about this match, and yet what we know is amply sufficient for judgment. We know that it lasted thirty-four years, and we know that after he lost his wife in 1920 this aggressive, confident, self-sufficient man was like a watch with the mainspring broken. The watch may look all right, and all its parts may seem to be there, but the wheels don't turn any more. He survived her by four years, but he was never the same man again. No more need be said about Lola Spencer Tanner; in fact, considering all that it implies, it is hard to think of anything finer that could be said about any wife.

Yet with all his success, in courtship as in business, Tanner was still dissatisfied. He was not quite where he wanted to be. At the same time, he was in a position in which various avenues were open to him and the fact that he chose the line he did reveals much about the man.

As an associate of Spencer he was favorably placed to continue in finance, with every hope of large success. The banker type would have taken that line. Yet if he felt it imperative to have something to do with cotton, the same association put him in a good position to pursue the career of a middleman, and his trading instinct would have helped immensely. It is easy to believe that if Tanner had been content with buying and selling —and all who knew him agree that his mercantile talent was highly developed—he would have become a figure of importance in the market, perhaps a very great shipper with international connections and a larger fortune than the one he acquired. The trader type would have taken that line.

Finally, it would seem that he was in a very nice spot from which to act in the futures market. It is doubtful that Spencer would have encouraged that, but there is no doubt that Tanner had the shrewdness and the nerve to make a very smart speculator. It is the swiftest of all ways to acquire money, as it is also the swiftest way to lose your shirt. A gambler would have taken that line.

Tanner, however, was a complex character. His success, as a young man, in discounting commercial paper indicates that he had the elements of a good banker in his make-up. His ability as a trader was one of the most conspicuous things about him. Finally, the brisk confidence with which he took chances that appalled other men certainly indicates that there was a streak of the gambler in him, and a pretty broad streak.

But there was another element in his character that must also be taken into account. Perhaps it was an inheritance from the Colonel, the old ironmaster. Perhaps it stemmed from his early experience when he worked with his father and watched the railroad line stretch out day after day, farther toward its appointed goal. At any rate, he liked to see things grow under his hand, he liked to produce something that he could see, and touch, and say, "This I made."

The banker and the middleman at most merely facilitate the work of the producer on the one hand and the manufacturer on the other. The speculator does even less—he profits most by other men's slowness and bad judgment. None of them can point to a definite, material object—a building, a railroad, a bale of cotton, a warehouse full of finished goods—and say, "This is my work." Tanner wanted to say it.

There is no evidence that he figured it all out this way, even in his own mind, and to others he always said that he turned to manufacturing solely because there was a larger future in it. For him, that was literally true because, for him, the larger future was not comprised entirely in larger profits. Manufacturing offered him interest, excitement, variety, a chance to exercise all his faculties, not merely those of shrewdness and alertness. It also involved harder work, heavier responsibility, and greater risks, but such considerations never deterred a strong man rejoicing in his strength.

There are people whose chief satisfaction in life seems to be gained from explaining away the ability of any successful man. In later years this type fell upon the association with Spencer to account for Tanner; the elder man, they said, was the real power and the younger merely his dutiful lieutenant.

It is a waste of time to argue against this sort of thing, because people who believe it are rarely open to argument and, in this case, there is a half-truth in the assertion. The relation with Spencer unquestionably was valuable to Tanner, least of all for the financial backing his father-in-law gave him. Spencer was a man of great ability and immense experience; his wise counsel must have been of inestimable value to the younger man and the fine personal relation between them must have multiplied that value. But although Paul sat at the feet of Gamaliel, Gamaliel wasn't Paul. The work that S. B. Tanner did in the world was not simply a continuation of the work that J. S. Spencer did. It was a different sort of creation, requiring for its accomplishment a different type of genius; and to deny all credit to the worker because he frequently accepted the wise advice of his elders is fantastic.

# 3

THE PLUNGE WAS TAKEN IN THE early months of 1887. Among the country merchants with whom Tanner had had business dealings as a traveling salesman was one R. R. Haynes, who owned the site of an old iron foundry in Rutherford County, North Carolina. The place, called High Shoals, was on Second Broad River, and was capable of developing water power of considerable extent. Although at the time it was fairly remote from any industrial development, land was cheap and labor plentiful, if unskilled. Haynes fell in with Tanner's plans and agreed to exchange his power site for stock in a textile manufacturing company.

Tanner put up $10,000 of his own and Spencer as much. Additional capital to the extent of $90,000 was raised in Charlotte with an ease that astonished and gratified Tanner. It was due to the fact that, while he had no experience in textile manufacturing, he did have a reputation for succeeding with whatever he undertook, and investors in those days were inclined to examine the man rather than the project.

Spencer was made president of the corporation, and Tanner was elected Lord High Everything-Else in reality, although his title on the books was Secretary-Treasurer. Cotton mill men in those early days were much given to the charming custom of naming new enterprises after feminine members of their families; so, in compliment to Mrs. Spencer, this one was called the Henrietta Mills. Ground was broken within two months after the original organization meeting, rather startling speed even for those days when the industry was letting no grass grow under its feet.

Now, at the age of thirty-five, Simpson Bobo Tanner entered upon his real career. Superficially, it seems that he had spent an inordinate length of time fumbling around, but actually it is doubtful that he lost a day. Every enterprise in which he had engaged during his first thirty-five years had contributed in some way to fit him for his main life's work. His boyhood days on the farm taught him about cotton and about North Carolina country people. His years as a salesman taught him about cotton and still more about country people. His free-lancing with the sheetings and shirtings taught him about cotton cloth and about the men who made and those who sold it. His association with Spencer taught him about cotton and about manufacturers and financiers. All the way along he had been learning things that it would be urgently necessary to know when he started manufacturing. He learned the hard way, but he learned thoroughly; possibly he might have acquired the information faster by some other form of schooling, but it is doubtful that he could have learned as well in any other way.

So he went to High Shoals inexperienced in certain techniques but nevertheless with a vast store of information; and of all that he knew perhaps the most valuable item was the certainty that you don't know any job until you know it from the ground up. Tanner started below that. He went not *to* the ground but *into* the ground with the construction gang that was digging the foundation. He saw the dirt that was thrown out of the trenches. He saw the rock on which the first course of bricks rested. He plodded through the mud with the mule-teams that were hauling in building material. He waded in the river with the crew that was preparing the footings for the dam.

He knew that mill from under the surface of the ground to the sealing coat that finished the top of the walls.

He encountered all the usual troubles that afflicted the early builders—inefficient labor, unskillful foremen, delayed and misdirected supplies, rock where no rock ought to be and soft mud where he had counted on rock, troubles and delays due to drought and troubles and delays due to floods.

But he overcame them all, and why he overcame them is suggested by a tale that his brother delighted in repeating for the rest of his life. In a temporary shack used as an office Simps Tanner was struggling with a mass of paper work when a sudden, violent rainstorm sent what in the West they call a "flash flood" down the river, threatening to carry away the half-finished dam and everything else. With one accord the workmen scampered for high ground where they stood around watching the boiling torrent, but Tanner never budged from his desk. Presently he summoned young Andrew to take a batch of messages to the telegraph office some distance away. Andrew found the office almost afloat, with water spurting through the cracks between the floor boards.

"Simps," said Andrew. "You better get out of here. What are you going to do if this shack goes?"

"Don't know," answered Simps, absently, still

studying the papers on his desk. "Go with it, I reckon."

To say that he would literally have gone with it if the shack had fetched away would be nonsense. He would have jumped, of course. But in a deeper sense it was perfectly true. If some financial, or technological, or political storm had swept away the Henrietta, Tanner would have gone with it, for he had thrown into the enterprise not only his money, but his skill, his intelligence, his hopes, his aspirations, his whole heart. And that is the strongest of all the reasons why it wasn't swept away.

On the contrary, it made money practically from the day the wheels first began to turn; within three years it was making big money; within seven years its return was terrific.

No attempt will be made here to trace, even in outline, the triumphant course of Henrietta Mills and all the allied enterprises that followed it, because this is a study, not of the economics of the textile industry, but of a human personality. Once a man has worked out the formula for success, the size of his success depends mainly on how long his health and strength hold out; and the first success is measured, not by its monetary return, but by the nature and size of the difficulties that had to be overcome to achieve it. It is easy to say that the Henrietta Mills succeeded because of an intelligent production policy backed by superfine salesmanship; but to explain to the modern generation what either meant is much more difficult.

For one thing, the word "intelligent" as applied to the production policy has, to a considerable extent, reversed its meaning in seventy years. That is to say, many things that were highly intelligent in 1887 would be absurd today. This is the stubborn fact that constantly trips writers of social history, especially those who are committed to a particular point of view. They cannot disabuse their minds of the delusion that what is intelligent (or just, or reasonable, or right in any way) today must necessarily be so tomorrow; and, on the contrary, that what is outrageous today must have been outrageous in 1887.

Consider, for example, S. B. Tanner's original labor policy, when the Henrietta Mills began operations. It was paternalistic to the last degree. He regulated, not merely the working conditions, but the private lives of his operatives to an extent that would drive modern labor to revolt in twenty-four hours.

Drinking, for example, was absolutely forbidden, not only on the job, but anywhere on the company property—and the company property included the village in which the operatives lived. Tanner fired his own brother twice for drinking, the second time unjustly, for he was cold sober and some spiteful person had been telling lies about him. But the incident shows the rigidity of the rule.

Disorderly conduct of course meant prompt expulsion from the place. Gambling was out. Profane swearing was not tolerated. Contemporaries delight in recalling one exception to this rule. A wagon hauling a heavy safe to the office sank hub-deep in the mud and the four-mule team simply quit. After all efforts had failed for a long time, a big Negro muleteer stepped up to Tanner and said he could get them out if the boss would permit him to use his own methods. Told to go ahead, he proceeded to "gee" and "haw" the team into a straight line, and then flew into lurid profanity. He cursed those mules collectively, he cursed them individually, he cursed them up one side and down the other, he swore until the air was blue and crackling. And the mules, hearing the voice of mastery, with one accord sank belly to earth, surged into the collars and yanked the wagon out of the mud.

"Hm-m-m," said Tanner, thoughtfully. "Looks like they really needed cussing, doesn't it?"

But he did not abrogate the rule.

Prostitution, needless to say, was ruthlessly extirpated, but the code of sexual morality covered more than commercialized vice. Men and women guilty, or even strongly suspected, of promiscuity regardless of the mercenary motive were banished; and parents who might be correct enough in their own lives but who permitted their children to create scandal soon found themselves out of a job, which meant out of the village. The peace officers were employes of the company, which meant that company regulations had the force of law.

All this sounds tyrannous, and latter-day writers have frequently portrayed it as abominable tyranny. In the records of Henrietta Mill village—and of a hundred others, for the system was more or less general—one with the mental slant of, say, the novelist Howard Fast, might easily find authentic material with which to paint a revolting picture. All that is necessary to make it monstrous is to omit all description of social conditions prevalent at the time.

But when all the relevant facts are brought into the picture it makes a very different impression. Not a heavenly impression, by any means—a hasty disavowal that is necessary because some apologists for the pioneer mill men have gone to the other extreme and have painted them as angels that they never were. The village system, like every other social system, was capable of being abused and at times was abused; and at best it had inherent defects that have brought about its abandonment to a large extent in recent years. But in 1887 it had the merit of meeting certain exigent requirements that could have been met in no other way.

To begin with, the original Henrietta mill, like many others at that time, was built in open country and the only labor supply available consisted of people with not one cent of free capital. This was long before the day of the automobile; so shelter within walking distance of the mill was imperatively necessary. North Carolina had not a single city and the towns were too small to have developed large real-estate operators interested in rental property. The only solution was company housing.

Next, the people who came to work in the original mills were almost to a man dwellers in the neighboring hills—small farmers, tenants, sharecroppers, who for a quarter of a century without the slightest break had been suffering under hard times that make the great depression of the thirties look almost luxurious by comparison. Life in those remote valleys and coves had touched a level of austerity all but inconceivable by our generation, and had remained there for a long period.

Basically, these people were of excellent racial stock, but the best human stock in the world subjected for many years to the brutalizing effect of isolation, ignorance, and grinding poverty, will sink in the scale of civilization. These people came, for the most part, from isolated homes far—often miles—from the nearest neighbor; so naturally they had no conception of the social discipline that is indispensable where people live huddled together, even if the community is no larger than a cotton-mill village.

Finally, there was no time for a slow and gradual transformation of social attitudes. This is a factor that is often overlooked, but it is extremely important to an understanding of what really happened. The Southern cotton factories, and especially those in North Carolina, were built with great rapidity. The investors had usually sunk most, if not all, their available capital in construction and in a majority of cases had incurred indebtedness to northern manufacturers of machinery. Therefore, it was urgently necessary for each new mill to get into operation at the earliest possible moment. Therefore, it was imperative for them to use whatever labor was at hand. Therefore, the labor had to preserve the decencies, if not the amenities, of civilized living in a relatively urban environment.

Sometimes the labor recruiting of the first textile manufacturers has been described in such a way as to suggest that the mill men plunged into the forest and rounded up hordes of savages little superior to the Kaffirs herded into the South African diamond mines. The suggestion is ridiculous, of course. These were civilized people, mostly English, Scotch, Irish, and German—heirs of a thousand years of western European culture. Their native intelligence was high and, as time has shown, they had their fair share of genius. They were not barbarians, but they were rustics compelled to become town-dwellers very suddenly and *en masse*.

If the mill towns had been able to absorb them gradually, family by family, the transition would have been far easier. In that case, each newcomer would have been surrounded by neighbors already accustomed to town ways and the change of habits and attitudes would have been almost automatic and comparatively easy.

But that was not the case. The villages were built in a single operation and populated all at once. Practically everybody had come in from the country, therefore there was no one to set fashions and establish customs. For large numbers of people to change their ways of living suddenly, and all together, is a rigorous requirement and rigorous measures were necessary to meet it.

In such circumstances what to outsiders resembles tyranny may be no more, in fact, than realistic dealing with an emergency. The proof that it was so regarded by the operatives is the fact that they submitted.

Critics of Southern industry have been guilty here of a curious self-contradiction. They have admitted, what is too well attested to be denied, that the Carolina hill people in their original environment were anything but an abject race. On the contrary, they were notoriously independent—stiff-necked, froward, lawless were terms frequently applied to them, but never meek and servile. Yet when they were assembled in the mill villages the companies had remarkably little trouble in enforcing sumptuary regulations of a very radical type.

The only possible explanation is that a majority of the people saw in the regulations nothing that was entirely unreasonable. They might object to a detail here and there, but they approved the system as a whole. It was the reaction of basically intelligent men. They knew that they did not understand this new environment and they assumed that the heads of the company did. So they obeyed even when they did not comprehend, and a huge rural population was urbanized out of hand with astonishingly little disturbance.

Few industrialists carried this operation through more successfully than S. B. Tanner. He was no sociologist and but little of a philosopher, yet he developed a social philosophy that when practically applied was so effective that his mills became famous as good places in which to work. Its development was purely empirical, if you delight in text-book terms; but it was empiricism colored—possibly distorted—by a definite point of view attributable to certain definite mental traits. To come down to the vernacular, if Tanner was no scientist or philosopher, neither was he a stuffed shirt.

To the end of his life nothing exasperated him more than to hear references to "the mill-hand class." To him the hands were not a class, they were simply people who happened to work in the mills, but otherwise exactly like the people who worked on farms, or in stores, or on railroads, or anywhere else that they could make a living. An old woman who had spent a large part of her life in Henrietta Mills described him, after his death, with unstudied but extraordinary clarity; she said, "He always treated us mill people like we was somebody."

To him they were somebody. To him they were just as good as anybody else. He really believed it, and the reality of his belief shone through everything he said and did. The result was that he could take the very hide off a mill hand—he had a scathing tongue when he chose to use it—and while the man might be vastly indignant he was not insulted. The boss was giving it to him, to be sure, but as man to man, not as lord to serf. That kind of dressing-down a man can take without any rankling feeling that his manhood has been impugned. The boss might be cantankerous, but, after all, he had fired his own brother for violating the rule against drinking; so you couldn't say that he thought of himself and his family as being elevated above other people. He was a bad man to monkey with, but he was a man, all right, and he didn't think himself a little tin god. So Tanner was able to maintain a discipline that an insincere man could never have managed.

It was his salvation in the situation that existed in 1887 and for twenty years thereafter. He was introducing modern technology to a population who had not the remotest conception of what it meant. With a raw, untrained labor force he was entering into competition with an old, highly-organized industry. He had to have discipline if he was to stand a chance. But it must be discipline, not mere domination. Discipline means obedience that is willing, as well as prompt. Slavish submission is no substitute, as had been proved when pre-Civil War slaveowners attempted to employ Negro labor in industry and failed dismally.

But true discipline is not established by a Simon

Legree. Only a leader, not a driver, can accomplish the task; and the first requisite of a leader is justice with no trace of condescension. A man who feels himself above the common herd can admit an inferior to his grace, but it is very hard for him to recognize the inferior's rights. Tanner admitted the existence of no inferiors—no superiors, either, but in dealing with his labor force the other side of the shield was the important one. He was no sentimentalist; he believed firmly that a man can, and frequently does, forfeit all his rights by his own misconduct, and he acted ruthlessly on that belief. But it never entered his mind to doubt that a man, including a millhand, has rights to begin with.

But this story would be definitely falsified were it to fail to mention at this point a factor which was in flat contradiction of the Tanner policy, yet contributed to his success to an extent that is unknown but certainly important. This was his wife. Lola Spencer Tanner felt no responsibility for administering justice among the mill people. Her field was mercy. Like most Southern ladies of her generation she let her husband's business severely alone; but pain of body and distress of mind among the villagers were her business, and in administering it she serenely ignored all his rules and regulations. When trouble came, she let him investigate the causes; she busied herself in palliating the sad results. She didn't mind being good to the undeserving, not in the least, and so she was adored.

In modern times the name "Lady Bountiful" has become a term of reproach, almost an epithet, among social workers; and not without reason, for a cold, touch-me-not charity is despicable. But while the gift of any material thing may under some circumstances be an insult, the gift of warm, genuine sympathy, however expressed, is now, as it always has been, the greatest amelioration of human existence. Lola Tanner knew how to give it to her people; and although she has been thirty years dead her memory is still radiant among those who survive.

It is a curious circumstance that one of Tanner's conspicuous successes in his labor policy was achieved by the very means through which some employers have reduced their workers to virtual peonage. This was the company store.

In the beginning it was, like the village itself, a plain necessity. The people had to be supplied, and as there was no one else to do it the company undertook the responsibility. Then, having set up a retail store on its own property, with its own capital, it naturally refused to admit competitors. In some places this system undoubtedly subjected the mill people to abominable extortion, for the company, supplying inferior goods at high prices, kept them perpetually in debt.

But Tanner was a merchant himself, a genuine merchant, not a mere measurer, wrapper, and change-maker. He was firmly convinced that the function of a store is to supply the customer with an attractive article, of good quality, at a price the customer can pay, and it galled him to be connected with any establishment that violated that rule. He saw to it that his company store should be a genuine mercantile establishment. That he succeeded is not a matter of hearsay; it is attested by the fact that within a very short time people not connected with Henrietta Mills were coming from miles around to make their purchases at the company store. Incidentally, far from being a drag on the company, as many such establishments were, it turned out to be startlingly lucrative; in its third year it turned in a large net profit, which materially assisted the company in its early struggles.

But the real backbone of the Tanner production policy, the thing that finally made his enterprises—for the Henrietta Mills, after being greatly expanded, were followed by others, Florence, Green River, Cleghorn, some built by Tanner and some rehabilitated by him after they had fallen into financial difficulties—was not any device of his but a sternly realistic appreciation of what could and what could not be done.

S. B. Tanner was sharply aware that the cream of the textile industry is the manufacture of fine fabrics, and he burned to break into that field; but his yearning never overcame his common sense. The elaborate, up-to-the-minute machinery required for that kind of work he might have managed, but it also required operatives with special skills that can be developed only by intensive training and long experience. These simply did not exist in the South in sufficient numbers to make that kind of operation practicable.

Accordingly, he proceeded to do what he could with the facilities that were available. This is deceptively simple in the statement. For a lethargic man, it is easy enough. He plods along in the old rut and as long as he makes money is quite content. But Tanner was a dynamo of energy, throwing off ideas like a shower of sparks. He saw with tantalizing clearness the possibilities of the manufacture of fine products, not only in the immediate profit, but also in the solidarity it would give the industry; so the fact that he resisted the temptation to undertake what he could not handle is a tribute to his extraordinary balance. All his life he talked about it. All his life he was scornful of those Southerners who whined about the unfair tactics of the New

England manufacturers, when the real advantage of New England, as Tanner saw it, was its ability, developed by generations of practice, to turn out finer goods than the Southern mills could produce. But with all his talk he never deceived himself about what he could do.

On the other hand, he missed no opportunity to improve the coarse goods that his people were capable of making. Very early he adopted as a trade mark the head of a mastiff, printed in blue, on the cotton cloth from Henrietta Mills; and very soon the trade discovered that "dog's head cloth" did not deteriorate but constantly improved in quality as the years passed.

Tanner knew all his mills from top to bottom, but the loom, the weave room, was his special interest. He knew that right there, following all the painstaking work that had gone into cotton selection, meticulous preparation, carding, and spinning into the finest possible quality of yarn, it was easy by careful attention to detail, rather than by any miracle-working new inventions, to make cloth of first quality; or, by careless work, to let it slip off into second-rate stuff.

It didn't slip. On the contrary, as his people increased in skill, the Tanner products steadily improved in quality; and that tendency made them easy to sell.

So much for the intelligent production policy. As for the other of the two chief elements in the success of the Tanner enterprises, superfine salesmanship, it too can be traced to the large humanity of the man.

There is, unquestionably, an activity called salesmanship that depends upon inhumanity. There are men who are appallingly learned in all that tends to make a human being something less than a man, the weaknesses, the ignorance, the fatuity, that afflict us all and overwhelm some of us. It is possible to make a profit by playing on these things; but that, although it is called salesmanship, is in fact part of the art, not of the salesman, but of the swindler.

But if the true salesman is, as Tanner and later Filene conceived him, a man whose function in the world is to supply people's real needs promptly, adequately, and at a price they can afford to pay, then the salesman must know his customer in his strength, as well as in his weakness. He must know the whole man; and no one ever did that who was less than a whole man himself.

This quality Tanner had demonstrated brilliantly long before he became a textile manufacturer. On the road he had proved himself not merely a good salesman but a very fine one indeed. What made him superfine, a genuinely great salesman, was not the acquisition of any new quality but merely his ability to extend to a tremendous field the qualities he already possessed.

It was noted on a preceding page that the mountain counties he had formerly covered in the Carolinas were rough country; but they were smoothness itself by comparison with Asia, Africa, South America and the remotest islands of the sea, which was the territory that Tanner boldly determined to cover. He could not traverse this territory with a horse and buggy. He could not traverse it in person at all. No man could. The world was too wide for that approach. But he believed that he could nevertheless learn to know it, and he did learn.

He never wavered in the belief that a man is a man, brown-skinned, yellow-skinned, black-skinned, or white, and that his needs are human needs. If you supply him adequately, promptly, at a price he can pay, you can do business with him, and whether the business is transacted on the banks of the Yadkin or of the Yangtze Kiang is a detail of secondary importance.

To supply human needs adequately, however, takes ingenuity. To make sure that the quality of the goods is satisfactory is the first, but only the first, consideration when you are dealing with dwellers in remote places. This had been burned into Tanner's mind in the days when he had been bumping over the incredibly bad roads of his mountain territory. The goods must somehow be laid down within the customer's reach, and the bill collector must be on the spot and able to make change.

The easy way would have been to find customers in easily accessible places, in London, Paris, Berlin. But the easy way was blocked off from the pioneer North Carolina manufacturers because they couldn't produce the goods such markets demanded. With their strong and serviceable but coarse goods, they had to go after people who needed such wares; and they were the swarming millions in the far reaches of Asia, Africa, and in the backwoods of South America.

This is why S. B. Tanner, in Rutherford County, North Carolina, presently became an expert on the geography of inner Manchuria. The time came when he knew the road from Rutherfordton to Charlotte hardly better than he knew the Silk Road, that immeasurably ancient highway that Marco Polo traveled. He knew the routes that the pack-trains followed out of Srinagar, in Kashmir, and he could tell you the maximum load that a bearer could transport over the route of the Five Great Passes. He knew no more—perhaps he knew less—about available water transportation on the

Mississippi than on the Nile, the Congo, and the Amur.

For such information was essential to his function as a salesman who delivered the goods. Not all manufacturers thought so; some were content to leave such studies to factors in New York, to whom they delivered the goods, and thought no more about them. But Tanner never worked that way. He dealt with commission houses, brokers, and all sorts of middlemen, to be sure, but they were his agents—he remained always the principal. He never scorned the advice of any man who knew whereof he spoke, but he was seldom obliged to take the word of any agent for anything. He knew. He pored over maps, guide-books, economic surveys, consular reports, and hundreds and thousands of pages of statistical tables.

One result was that he foresaw the inevitable loss of the Manchurian market to the Japanese long before many of his competitors understood it, and he took measures to transfer his own operations to other areas well in time.

In one way this tremendous store of information contributed to his unhappiness. Because he understood the economics of the Far Eastern trade so thoroughly, he saw with distressing clarity every mistake that the United States government made in the Orient. Our lack of satisfactory banking facilities, in particular, he bewailed for years. It meant that his bill collector frequently had difficulty in making change. In Polk County it might be a matter of a few dollars, in Manchuria hundreds of thousands, but the principle was the same. When he could not interest the government in the problem, he turned to the great New York banks. There he accomplished something, but never as much as he hoped, or as much as he thought essential to the consolidation of our position.

In this he may have been wrong. He was perpetually comparing our lethargy with the activity of the British, whose great financial institutions in Hong Kong were the model of what Tanner thought we ought to do. Yet, as the event proved, the excellent British financial connections in China did not save them when the crash came, and similar connections probably would not have saved us. Tanner's information on political conditions was not to be compared with his knowledge of the economic situation. But no man can know everything; if we had had political experts who knew their stuff as well as S. B. Tanner knew his, experts who could have instructed him in politics and in turn learned from him trade conditions, among them they might have made our relations with China a different and much happier story.

But that is water over the dam now. This story

is concerned, not with what might have been, but what was; and what actually happened was that the demands of his business forced S. B. Tanner to lift his mental horizon again and again, to abandon parochial, and provincial, and even nationalistic ways of thinking until the sometime country boy became first a North Carolinian, then a Southerner, then an American, and eventually a citizen of the world, perceiving that the fortunes of men are so curiously linked together that what happened in Henrietta mill village might have an effect in some thatch-and-wattle hamlet on the shores of Lake Chad, or where the felt yurtas are grouped in High Tartary.

Something of the sort happened also to some of his contemporaries—not all, for not all of the original textile barons owed their success chiefly to great salesmanship. There was D. A. Tompkins, for example, with his intense interest in the technology of textile manufacturing, who was doubtless a better production man than Tanner; and there was Stuart W. Cramer, with his sorcerer's ability to make capital appear apparently out of thin air, who was a better financier. Each led a considerable group, as Tanner led the great salesmen; and the technical men and the financiers were not compelled to look abroad to the same extent that the salesmen were.

Nevertheless, there were enough of the Tanner type to have an appreciable effect on the thinking of the entire industry, and, through the industry, on the mentality of the state. A peculiarity in the thinking of North Carolina, especially in the first half of the twentieth century, has been noted by many outside observers, most keenly, perhaps, by Arnold J. Toynbee, the English historian. In the fourth volume of his gigantic *Study of History*, is an arresting passage in which he contrasts the thinking of North Carolina with that of her neighbor states to the north and south; in North Carolina, he observed, people thought outward and forward, rather than inward and backward, as they did in Virginia and South Carolina.

Toynbee accounted for this difference by the assumption that North Carolina did not have so far to fall when the Civil War hit the South, and so was able to climb back sooner. But a theory at least as plausible is that among the business leaders of the state were numbers who were racking their brains trying to understand the preferences and prejudices of customers in Bombay and Mozambique, and devising means of delivering goods there in perfect condition and conveniently packed. Such men had to think outward and forward during business hours; surely, it was natural for them to continue the same habit of thought when they turned to other interests—to education, to politics, to public works, to philanthropy. It so happens that the other great industry of North Carolina, tobacco manufacture, also operates in a world market. Together, they could hardly fail to broaden the outlook of the commonwealth as a whole.

In 1908 Tanner served as President of the American Cotton Manufacturers' Association, and the presidential address he prepared for the meeting in Richmond on May 20 of that year is the only extended writing that he left. It is interesting, not for the specific ideas advanced, most of which were long ago either adopted or outmoded by changing conditions, but for the spirit in which the speaker attacked the problems. It was a year of depression, a sharp "bankers' panic" having thrown business into the doldrums the preceding autumn; so the address naturally was devoted in large part to consideration of that situation.

Tanner was a political conservative, what impatient liberals called "a hide-bound conservative." Nevertheless, the significant part of this address is a call for action, action, and again action! Conservative he may have been, but not inert. He wanted ship subsidies; he wanted the financial buccaneers who had precipitated the panic restrained by law; he wanted the tariff brought, if not into a sound, at least into a sane, relation to economic fact; he wanted rational currency legislation; he wanted railroad regulation that would regulate; deploring the political rat-race in Washington, he demanded that Congress give to the economic interests of the country an amount of attention not far short of a planned economy.

True, after proposing this tremendous upheaval in the whole economic and juristic system, he wound up by throwing a sop to the perpetually terrified, in the form of the cliché that the country needed above all a period of quiet recovery.

But that was merely a bow to the conventions. Tanner was the last man to be interested in quietude. Nobody knew better than he that

> gardens are not made
> By singing, "Oh, how beautiful!"
> And sitting in the shade.

So the one formal record of his thought, the one time in his seventy-one years that he expressed himself in words on paper is essentially the thought of the young Tanner on the road forty years before—don't wait for the business, go after it; harness up by lantern light and let sunrise discover you well along the road to the place where the customer is to be found.

# 4

SIMPSON BOBO TANNER DIED ON JULY 3, 1924. The medical cause of death apparently was a cerebral hemorrhage suffered in 1923, but those who knew him best believe that the real stroke was the death of Mrs. Tanner, in 1920. He never got over that blow and its effect was redoubled in 1923 by the death of his youngest son, Spencer, in an automobile accident. This opinion may be correct, yet one suspects that it was colored somewhat by the feeling that nothing could extinguish this tremendous vitality except failure of the will to live. To connect S. B. Tanner with feebleness of any sort is difficult for those who knew him at the height of his power, and the fact that he had reached the age of seventy-one doesn't impress them; if he had really desired to live, had made up his mind to live, they cannot quite admit that even age could have broken that iron determination.

Fantasy? Self-deception? Superstition? Perhaps so, but of a very familiar sort. It accounts for the title conferred upon Tanner and his fellow-manufacturers by popular consent. They were called textile barons, and the title was appropriate, for, like the barons of feudal times, they not only owned, they ruled.

Among them were some who are to be classed with those holders of castles along the Rhine in the Middle Ages; they were robber barons, and their sensational exploits have attracted greater attention than the more important work of quieter men. But they were not typical. The baron who made history was a man who brought order out of chaos, who in return for service sheltered and protected his people, who built great works, established the reign of law, and laid the foundations for a finer civilization than he could create.

These nineteenth-century cotton mill men qualified. Barons they were in fact, if not in heraldry, and their lives and work were so important a part of the history of the South that the region cannot be understood unless they are taken into account. S. B. Tanner has been studied here as representative of the type. That is why there is so little of his personal history in these pages. His strictly individual wars and loves and tastes and desires might be interesting to a psychologist, and might be entertaining to a romantic, but they mean nothing to the world now that he has been dead for a quarter of a century. His work, on the contrary, does. The industry he helped create has profoundly modified North Carolina, not merely in its economy, but in all its ways of thinking and acting and living.

One reason for this is the fact that he was a constructor of men as well as of mills. Tanner had no faith whatever in industrial democracy, but he had great faith in industrial justice. Under no circumstances would he sell an employe stock in his enterprises. He had no objection to paying high salaries to exceptionally valuable men, but there was no taking them into partnership. At the same time, he thought it both wrong and foolish to try to hold a good man down. Time after time he encouraged his best men to go into business on their own account, even when their business would compete with his. He went further. Again and again he put up his own money to help them get started, buying stock in their new companies and sometimes serving as a director.

In the long run he lost nothing by this. Now and then death, or some other catastrophe, intervened and caused him to lose an investment, but he was never known to back a fool. Most of the men he helped get started made good in a big way and Tanner's venture paid off handsomely. But, what is more to the purpose of this study, this custom spread his influence far beyond the borders of his own property. Men whom Tanner had trained and helped were strewn throughout the textile industry and helped put his impress upon corporations in which he never owned a share of stock.

This is not to be construed as an assertion that he was invariably successful in human relations. He and one of his original partners, R. R. Haynes, who had owned the site of the first mill, quarreled, and there grew up in Rutherford County a legend of a blood-feud fit to make the quarrel of the Montagues and the Capulets look like a polite difference of opinion. This was more folklore than fact. Tanner and Haynes did disagree, and there is some evidence that each made pious and persistent efforts to skin the other in business deals. But the notion that each thirsted for the other's heart's blood is sheer melodrama. The truth seems to be that Haynes was simply too tough a nut for Tanner to crack. However, the incident does show that the man was not capable of getting along with everybody. S. B. Tanner was thoroughly human, with plenty of human failings.

For one thing, he stuck to his paternalistic labor policy long after it was outmoded. At the same time, he could make it work when younger men could not. After the enterprises had grown too big for his personal supervision, and he was spending much of his time in Charlotte and New York, he was sent for whenever labor trouble became really threatening. The record shows that without exception he went to the spot, spent a day, or three or four days, seeming to do nothing, and yet somehow the difficulty melted away. There was not a single strike at Henrietta as long as he was connected with the mill, and no really long, disastrous strike at any of the others.

"How did you do it? What is your method?" contemporaries were always asking him, and he was quite sincerely at a loss for a reply.

He was not conscious of having any method. In fact, he didn't have a method. What he had was a reputation, built up during the long years when he was actively superintending everything. In that time he had acquired the name of being hard but fair. Therefore his men had the idea that if they could only get to the boss and lay the whole situation before him, he would do what was right. So when he showed up in a time of trouble they would talk to him with a frankness they would not risk with anyone else. They were certain that if they were candid with him he would not use their candor to put them in the wrong.

The upshot was that it usually took him only a few hours to find out what was really at the bottom of the uproar. If the grievance was real, he redressed it, promptly and without argument. If the grievance was purely imaginary, he had a wonderful ability to show the men that it was imaginary. But if—and this was the most common and the most troublesome of labor conflicts—the grievance was real enough but was due to circumstances over which the company had no control, he might have to spend two or three days explaining all the complications before the men got the idea. In the end, however, they always got it, and as long as he lived the Tanner enterprises never had a long, bitter, and fruitless labor war.

This sort of adjustment by personal contact is, always was, and always will be the finest of labor policies; but unhappily its practical application is severely limited. When an organization attains a certain size it is impossible for the man with authority enough to commit the company to make personal contact with more than a small percentage of his workmen; so contact by representation is the only way out.

S. B. Tanner was well advanced in years before his companies got so big that personal contact was impracticable. In fact, it never became impracticable as far as he was concerned, simply because his reputation multiplied his bargaining efficiency manyfold. So he never understood the necessity of new methods of dealing with labor, and died suspecting that the new methods were not really necessary but were devices of self-seeking labor leaders to increase their importance and influence. Many of his contemporaries labored under the same handicap; and this has given the whole group the reputation of secretly yearning to establish peonage, when they were, in fact, enlightened and reasonable men merely handicapped by the human tendency to cling to what we have learned in youth even though conditions have changed as age has crept upon us.

Tanner's reputation, of course, multiplied his effectiveness in many situations other than labor disputes. When he was at the height of his powers, having come into control of half a dozen vast establishments, he decided that he was carrying too heavy a load, and sold his holdings in the Henrietta Mills. A few years later a combination of bad luck and bad management got the company into a financial jam so serious that the creditors came swarming in for the kill. The management appealed to Tanner, who re-bought enough shares to qualify as a director and took over. The crisis disappeared. Yet it is apparent from the record that he did not do one hand's turn toward solving it. The trouble was that the mills' credit had been exhausted; yet when word went around that S. B. Tanner was in control again, immediately the mills had all the credit they could possibly need, and before he had time to hang up his hat in the office there was no crisis to be solved.

Such matters are, however, facets of an individual personality, and the effort here has been to present not a personality, however interesting or however admirable, but the representative of a type—not Tanner the citizen, husband, father, neighbor, and friend; but Tanner the textile baron, because it was the textile barons who profoundly modified the state of North Carolina, and who still influence it.

There is, however, one personal attitude that demands attention, even in a more or less impersonal study. S. B. Tanner, like some, but not all, of his colleagues habitually voted the Democratic ticket when election day came around.

For this he has been accused of hypocrisy. He believed in the gold standard. He believed, with modifications, in the protective tariff. He accepted, again with modifications, the doctrine of *laissez faire*. He advocated strongly business in government, while violently opposing government in business. In short, he was more rather than less conservative in his views than Grover Cleveland, and the ideas of William Jennings Bryan seemed to him lunacy. All this would seem to make him, in the years before the first World War, the very model of a stout Republican. Nevertheless, he usually voted Democratic.

Hasty and superficial observers have explained this hastily and superficially by saying that such men—for Tanner was not the only one—were cynics who attached no weight to the citizen's responsibility to vote his convictions. But the explanation fails to hold water, because most of them were not cynical about anything else. On the contrary, it was precisely the few who were obviously cynics who did vote Republican.

The answer deserves much more careful analysis than can be given it here, for it is to be found in the obscure region of conflicting loyalties. This is an area of American political behavior that has never been sufficiently explored, but that is important because it is national, not regional. It is as conspicuous in Maine and Vermont and Kansas as it ever was in the South, and one must take it into account in explaining anything the American democracy does.

Unquestionably, Tanner felt that he owed a

duty to his state and his section that overrode his duty to himself and his business interests. The play of tremendous and tremendously complicated historical forces over a period of many years had fixed in his mind the conviction that voting the Republican ticket meant subjecting the Southern states to the danger of coercion, not merely economic, but social. Whether this conviction was true or false is irrelevant for this discussion; the point is that Tanner held it, and as long as he held it he was bound to infer that while Republican rule would be better for business, it would be worse for society in the state of North Carolina; and when he went to the polls he put his social duty ahead of his business interests.

But this isn't cynicism, this is idealism, of a very potent variety. Let it be repeated for emphasis—he may have been entirely wrong in his estimate of the situation; but as long as it was his estimate, his conduct was not blameworthy, it was admirable.

So let us mark the score *da capo*, and return to the beginning: Simpson Bobo Tanner did none of the things that schoolboys think are necessary to make a man a historical figure. But he made history. Because he and his like lived and labored in those years between the end of the Civil War and the beginning of the new century, North Carolina is different and all who live in the state have had a different experience. Romantic souls there are who wail that the difference is all for the worse, that because life is easier men are softer, that those who work at machines have become machines, robots, soulless, mindless, hopeless. We are all regimented, we are all reduced to a dead level, and a new Swinburne might say of industrialization, "the world has grown gray at thy breath."

Well, if it is so, it is because we have not looked into the pit whence we were digged. For this industry that is supposed to have abolished manly virtue was itself the product of manly virtue—of courage, of endurance, of resourcefulness, of grim resolution. Maybe there were touches of ferocity in the process, perhaps some tyranny and oppression were involved; but if there were vices, they were masculine vices, nothing soft, nothing weak, nothing epicene. The barons did not become barons by kneeling on a velvet carpet to be touched with the Sword of Honor; they came by the title in the old, stern way, through "blood, toil, sweat and tears," not by sycophancy and boudoir influence. If so virile a process has produced effeminacy, then we are in the presence of a miracle.

It is not true. If degeneration threatens, it is not because of what they did, it is because of our failure to comprehend what they did. Their ideas are outmoded, for the nineteenth century is fifty years in the past. Their mistakes are glaringly plain. But the point is that neither the ideas nor the mistakes did the work. Other ideas might have served as well, and if they had been adopted other mistakes would have been made. Neither can serve as a guide to this generation, for each must evolve its own ideas and make its own mistakes.

The things that counted were the high heart, the iron will, and the courage that fatigue, frustration, and despair could not bend. They are not outmoded and they can serve as guides for this or any other generation.

Simpson Bobo Tanner perhaps would have derided this description of him and his fellows, for he was a matter-of-fact man. But one of the attractive traits of the early Southern industrialists is that they seldom gave themselves credit for their best work. They firmly believed that they had saved thousands of people from starving, and they plumed themselves on having brought to the state vast material wealth. But that they had set for it a new standard of courage and endurance rarely, if ever, occurred to them. Yet the fact that by Southern brains and Southern grit the South was dragged out of the Slough of Despond is a heritage of greater value than material wealth "for riches certainly make themselves wings; they fly away as an eagle toward heaven," but the splendor of a great achievement is a treasure that abides, yesterday, today, and forever.

www.ingramcontent.com/pod-product-compliance
Lightning Source LLC
Chambersburg PA
CBHW031714230426
43668CB00006B/210